Silver in the Fie

'er'

summer

buttercups

clover

Silver

flowers

other

another

under

It was a sunny day in the summer. Poppies, buttercups, daisies and clover were in the fields next to the wood.

Silver, the rabbit, was eating the grass among the flowers. Suddenly she heard a gunshot.
Bang!

Silver ran under the hedge. Her heart was thumping, thump, thump, thump. She was scared.

Silver waited in the hedge. She listened until everything was quiet. She peeped out from the hedge.

Then she ran across the field. She heard another gunshot. **Bang!** Silver fell under the hedge at the other side of the field.

Silver's heart was thumping, thump, thump, thump. She was scared. She stayed very still under the hedge.

Silver waited in the hedge until everything was quiet again. She was scared, but she wanted to get back to her burrow.

She hopped along the edge of the field staying under the hedge. At last she saw the trees at the edge of the wood.

She ran across the grass to her burrow under the big tree. She quickly disappeared down it.

Soon she was deep in her burrow. She was not scared now. She was safe. She went to sleep.

Vowels:
- ai/ay/a-e: day daisies waited stayed staying again safe
- ee/ea/ie: peeped trees deep sleep eating field
- ow/o/: burrow clover
- oo: soon
- oo: wood
- ow/ou: down out now
- er: summer buttercups Silver flowers clover under another other
- er/ear: her heard
- aw: saw
- ear: disappeared
- -y: sunny suddenly quickly very
- -ies: poppies daisies
- soft g: hedge edge

Verbs:
- -ed verbs: listened peeped stayed waited wanted hopped disappeared scared
- Others: was were ran heard saw went fell

Exceptions: everything among quiet heart